STORYTELLING

How to Write an Inspiring Memoir,

Oral History, or Family Genealogy

Manufactured in the United States of America.

Published by Our American Stories ® LLC
Tucson, Arizona
www.OurAmericanStories.com

ISBN 978-0-9862364-0-2
First edition, first printing

Book design and layout by G. David Thayer, Rapidsoft Press ®
Cover design by Peri-Poloni Gabriel, Knockout Design

Dedication

Stan and Kris at home in Sausalito, California, about 1949.

To my dear departed father, Stanton Delaplane, who raised me on pure oral history, telling me the stories of our ancestors year after year. Little did you know the spark that you were lighting for me. Thanks to you, I can pass this on so that other families will not lose their family history and that special connection with their ancestors.

Stanton Delaplane and his daughter, Kristin Delaplane, in Ireland ca 1957 –1958. Stan is holding an Irish Coffee. He was noted for introducing Irish Coffee to the United States at the Buena Vista Café in San Francisco. A plaque outside the café attests to that. As a reporter for the *San Francisco Chronicle*, Stan was awarded the Pulitzer Prize in 1942. He wrote an internationally syndicated travel, family, and humor column from 1953 to 1988, writing his last column the day before he died at age eighty.

Table of Contents

Preface

My mother died unexpectedly. I thought I had years left to ask her all those questions I wanted to ask her. It wasn't that I didn't want to sit down and talk to her about her life. It was because I didn't think she was going anywhere. There's a lot of stuff I'm never going to know.
—Stevie Nicks, singer, from the OWN channel's *Master Class* program

OUR LIFE JOURNEY and those journeys of our ancestors are the stories we are given to tell. However, when one is looking to chronicle the family history, a written memoir is not always considered. Regrettably, it is usually after someone dies that the family realizes the loss in not capturing that person's life story. Suddenly they have questions, and now no one is there to answer those questions.

Memoirs are family history. Imagine if you could go to your bookshelf today and pull down the memoir written by your great-great-grandfather. That is your history. Now imagine your great-great-granddaughter pulling down your memoir.

These life stories make for a deepening of the family's connection through the understanding of an individual from the challenges, failures, and successes they had. Strong connections of strength and wisdom are also made with the ancestors as their life experiences are revealed. Knowing that these life stories will continue to be passed down through the generations, the connection of the tribe is seen as ongoing.

Children love to hear the stories about their parents' and grandparents' lives over and over again, as well as the tales about their ancestors. Bruce Feiler, author and *New York Times* family columnist, states in his book, Secrets of Happy Families, that current research shows that knowing the family history is a significant predictor of a child's emotional well-being. Children who know about their parents, grandparents, and other relatives— their ups and their downs—have greater confidence when facing their own challenges. These stories give shape to and pass on the values, character, and spirit of a family. Family traits, idiosyncrasies, behaviors, and talents are revealed. Individual family members may gain a sense of what they can do and become. And, perhaps, what they might avoid—the family traps!

These life stories can also go a long way in healing relationships by awakening compassion. More than once, I have recorded a life story where the child or grandchild has said what a wonderful gift it was because now they understood the person so much better. In 1991, 100-year-old Lillie Cochrane Giles and I collaborated on her book, which consisted of her memoir and knowledge of her family's history. When the book was completed, the family held an autograph party at the town's senior center. In this room, her granddaughter said something so meaningful that I have never forgotten it: "I've known this woman all my life, and yet I didn't really know her." For me, this statement was all the more relevant because she had always lived with her grandmother. It shows how much modern-day life has cut into family storytelling and how little most of us really know about our own family members. Talk show host and media entrepreneur Oprah Winfrey beautifully expressed this need to be heard and the impact storytelling can have when she said all people have these thoughts in common: "Do you see me? Do you hear me? Does anything I say mean anything to you?"

If you have this book in your hand, then you're likely at the stage where you want to write a memoir about your life, or the lives of your parents or grandparents and the stories about your ancestors. My intention is to show you how to tell these stories. This guide will help you to decide what the story is about, conduct the necessary research, gather the relevant family photos and memorabilia, and write the book itself in an entertaining and inspiring manner.

The resources for your history may be your own recollections, senior family members whose memories you want to tap, family papers and photographs that you need to sort through, or the untapped research resources that you want to explore, such as online search tools like Ancestry.com.

I've explored family history books in the marketplace and haven't found one that encompasses this subject with all the elements you will find in this book. There are books on writing a family history and books on writing memoirs. But I think it's fair to say books that cover the subject from A to Z are not in the majority. I hope you will find I have come close to accomplishing that and, mainly, that your needs are addressed.

A special acknowledgment to Alan Rinzler, my editorial consultant, who suggested the direction and structure of the vast material I put at his doorstep. I want to thank G. David Thayer of Rapidsoft Press in Sarasota, Florida, who has taught me all I know about making a book from formatting to design to publishing options. David is also my seventh cousin, whom I met when he was crafting The *Delaplaines of America* genealogy back in the late '90s. Also, thanks to Maxine Ludeke, who is a genealogist in Tucson, Arizona. Maxine provided much of the information on researching genealogy from her talk, "Overcoming Brick Walls."

I've been conducting online and in-person trainings, workshops, and classes about writing memoirs for close to twenty-five years. I've had experience, therefore, preparing class curriculum and developing handouts. Most importantly, my students supplied me with a wealth of knowledge on the challenges they encountered, including what didn't work for them. I have also produced a number of memoirs and family history books for clients and so have that hands-on experience to tap that I now pass on to you.

Part One in this book focuses on writing about another family member, and Part Two is about writing about yourself. However, there are tips and tools in both sections can be applied to either scenario, so please be sure to look at both sections no matter what your goal is. Let's get started.

Kristin Moore Delaplane
Tucson, Arizona, 2015

Part One

Writing About Another Family Member

Chapter One

Getting Started

My Noni, which is "grandmother" in Italian, died when I was in my mid-
thirties, and I would have so many questions for her now. About her
childhood: When she moved out of Italy? Why did she move out of
Italy? Who were her parents, who were my great grandparents?
　　　　　　　　—Valerie Bertinelli in *Who Do You Think You Are?*

Do you have a grandmother from Italy who came over dec-
ades before you were born to live in the USA? Or a great grandmother from the countryside east of Stockholm who braved the
North Atlantic seas as a young woman to settle in Minnesota in
1867 and then build a prosperous family farm? Or a grandfather
who came over from Ulster as a strapping young lad and worked
himself up to the rank of detective sergeant in the City of New
York Police Department?

Do you have questions you wish you could ask these folks
directly, but alas, they're long gone? Well, it will take extensive
research, but you can, in fact, write their memoir. Or you can
craft a memoir of a living family relative so that you can ask the
questions now.

Begin by answering these questions:

Motivation

1. Why have you picked this specific individual?
2. What is it about this person that's inspired you to make this choice?

Research

1. When was this family member born?
2. Did they write any letters that have been preserved?
3. Are there any photographs?
4. Who's alive now who has any first-hand knowledge of this person?
5. Could there be a hand-written or even tape-recorded interview with this person available?

Next, take an inventory of what you have and what you still need. How can you begin to gather any missing materials? Here are some things to try:

1. Use the Internet to research the historical period of the individual's life from the time of their birth to death. Do not just use *Wikipedia*; there are undoubtedly specialized websites related to the place, profession, or historical events that were a part of your subject's life. For example, there's a lot of information available about the Finnish/ Swedish Famine of 1866–1868 that motivated that great grandmother from Sweden to set off for the USA.

2. Genealogy sites like Ancestry.com and FamilySearch.com provide a wealth of potential information, including existing family histories; stories and photographs; census data; military records; wills; and birth, marriage, and death records. LibertyEllisFoundation.org, FindaGrave.com, and Newspapers.com provide specialized information. (*See Chapter Seven for more detail on genealogy research.*)

3. Library archives for histories and biographies that cover the period and events during your subject's life, as well as any magazine, newspaper, or journal articles. For example, there are many books that focus on the role of the Irish police in New York City.

4. Oral histories gathered by special groups, such as Scottish, Irish, or Italian ethnic organizations, or Holocaust survivor organizations. Search local historical societies and church archives.

Evoking Important Memories

If you are going to interview someone for their life story, you need to help them with their memories.

Try to find a newspaper from the person's hometown dated around the time their family was there. Look just at the ads. From those you can get an idea of what was going on and possibly come up with some topics that will elicit memories and key stories.

Have them draw a diagram of the home and make a map of the neighborhood or town where they grew up. It is amazing how this simple exercise can fill the head with memories.

Timelines are invaluable as memory tools. Set up a timeline for their life and have them fill in events. Here is a brief example.

Date	Event
1936	Birth
1941	Started school
1945	Moved to Little Rock

(*See Appendix A, page 71, for some general topic ideas that may evoke memories.*)

At this point, stop and study all of your materials, keeping in mind the answers to the first two questions.

1. Why have you picked this specific individual?
2. What is it about this person that's inspired you to make this choice?

To give your readers an answer to these two questions, I suggest they begin the book with a preface that starts with something like "I originally started this book about my great-great-grandmother Christina Dingler Messeth because I wanted to know why and how she came to New York from Austria in 1858 at the age of twenty and then made her way via the Isthmus of Panama to San Francisco. It seems like such a daunting and courageous journey."

Keep in mind that this preface can address your own family as the only potential readers or, if you think the individual warrants a broader market of readers beyond just your family, write as if you're addressing anyone, anywhere. But always explain why you are doing this, for example: "If it weren't for my great uncle, no one would be getting vaccinated against polio today."

Planning

Next, begin to make a plan for the structure of the book. Organize the book into chapters with three or four scenes in each chapter. Consider precisely when in time to begin the book. Starting at the actual beginning is not necessarily the best place to catch the reader's attention and interest to keep going.

Whether the potential reader is your grandchild or a reader standing in a bookstore scrolling through the first pages, it's crucial to start with something sufficiently dramatic, a climactic moment like landing in the USA penniless, striking gold in California, leaving a farm in the dead of night to avoid paying the rent, or becoming the head of a successful organization. Start with a moment of struggle, a turning point, or an ultimate success.

Having started with this climactic moment, your narrative will now move back to the beginning, the back story: birth, parents, growing up. Organize the scenes and events so that the story proceeds in chronological order right through your opening scene and past it towards the end.

This end, by the way, should bring down the curtain when this particular story is over, when the original reason—your motivation for telling this story—has been achieved. For example, such an emotional landing place could be when success in some endeavor has been reached, or when an immigrant ancestor arrives at his destination. Or it could be at his death. Once you've made this plan, begin to implement these steps:

1. Make a list of everyone still alive who knew this family member or has stories to pass down about the ancestor. Include family, friends, and working associates.

2. Interview them.

Since interviewing may to be a major part of writing a memoir about another family member, let's take a careful look at that skill.

Chapter Two

How to Conduct an Oral History Interview

I always wanted to chronicle the family history with my mother. I wanted some researchers I'd worked with to talk to my mother, but, while interested, she was a little antsy about it. I know she would have gotten into it . . . But I wasn't forceful and didn't make it happen. That's one regret I have. I didn't get as much of the family history as I could have for the kids.

—Robert De Niro. *Esquire Magazine,* January 2003

PERHAPS YOU'VE ASKED your parents or grandparents to write about their life and their recollections of the ancestors. Unfortunately, this approach rarely yields good results. The parent or grandparent may express a willingness—may even have a desire to do this—but when it comes to the actual doing, it seems overwhelming or too time consuming, and the effort gets scattered to the wind.

Some people have delivered a digital recorder to a parent or grandparent, thinking this will be easier for them than writing. The problem with this approach is that you are not providing them with an audience. Most of us revel in being asked about our experiences and telling our stories. But sitting in an empty room talking to oneself is a whole other ballgame. And even if they tell the stories into a recorder in an empty room, the outcome will never be as lively or have as much detail as if they had that audience.

What is usually successful is the oral history approach. It is in this environment—where someone is completely captivated as the listener—that a person can ramp up their storytelling skills.

Equipment

We all love video, but oral history projects tend to be lengthy. The telling of a life story is from seven to ten hours, on average. That's a lot of video to watch. However, many of my clients have requested some video, so this is what I do. I start out by conducting a one-hour overview interview session that we videotape as well as capture on audio. You can do this by hiring a professional, or you can use something as simple as a cell phone and export that digital file into your computer. After that one-hour session, I segue to the audio recordings for the more detailed interviews.

For my audio recordings, I use a Marantz digital audio recorder and two lavalier microphones, one for me and one for the storyteller. Lavalier microphones are also known as clip mics because they clip onto clothing. My equipment is at the high end, but there are plenty of decent digital audio recorders that will give you good quality. The one thing you want to make sure of is that you can transfer the audio files from the recorder to your computer. And you do not want stereo for voice recordings; mono is the setting you want. My students have used the Olympus VN-721PC and VN-722PC, the difference being the amount of storage. They sell for between $50 and $70.

Interviewing via phone or over the computer using a service such as Skype.com is an only-if-I-have-no-other-choice option for me, because you lose a connection that is only there with a face-to-face interview. And another consideration is that the quality of the audio will not stand up to what you achieve when you are in the same room. Nevertheless, if no other option is available, a phone or computer program can provide a useful method of gathering information and stories. It is certainly better than nothing.

Always test your equipment the night before you conduct your interview. Once you arrive at the interview location, set up your equipment and test it again. Listen to the test audio and make sure you are picking up both voices and that no outside noises are interfering.

Setting

Try to interview the storyteller without anyone else in the room. Interviewing a husband and wife together is generally a poor idea because in most relationships there is a dominant speaker. Don't conduct these interviews at family gatherings. With all the extraneous noise, you'll wind up with a very poor recording, and many won't want to be taken off to a quiet place where they'll miss out on the family gathering.

The best place to conduct your interviews is where the storyteller feels most relaxed, like a room in their home. In advance of the interview, clarify that there will be no interruptions, such as phone calls, people wandering in the room, or observers.

Interviewing outdoors is not advised no matter how idyllic the setting. There are noises to which we are so accustomed they go unnoticed, but on a recorder they become very apparent, like a plane flying overhead. Don't interview anyone in a car. Chairs that rock or roll can be problematic, as can overstuffed furniture that the subject and microphone get lost in. These are a few things for you to be alert to.

One good setting for an interview is a dining room table. There is room to look at photographs or other family history material together, and you will have space to set out the recording equipment.

Wherever you choose, make certain there isn't any background noise such as radios, TVs, panting dogs, the sounds of people cleaning the house or washing dishes, or being directly next to a refrigerator or air conditioning unit. Avoid having cups and saucers or crunchy cookies on the table. It is amazing how loud the sound of a cup being set on a saucer comes across on a recorder. It would be a tragedy to lose that very important word or bit of a statement due to that nice cup of tea.

Take notes during the interview for possible follow-up questions or unusual spellings that you'll want to ask about later. On the occasions that the storyteller makes a notable non-verbal gesture or tears up or seems nervous, jot that down. These notations are a gold mine when you are developing a storyline from the recordings. Physical responses should always be noted in the transcript as well. Be sure to explain about your note taking in advance as the storyteller might become anxious wondering what your notes may mean.

Record for only about one and a half hours at a time. While the storyteller may be able to talk on, your listening skills will wane. With a break for lunch, two sessions a day works nicely.

Starting

Since you're making a record for future generations and maybe for a historical depository, you need to make sure people listening to this in the future can identify what they are listening to. Many oral history recordings at libraries or history centers have no identification as part of the recording. There may be a label attached, but that's not sufficient. What if the label fades or falls off? So this is how you do it: create an introduction script and read it directly into the recording. With a script you won't miss any of the points.

At the start of the first recording, say something like this:

a) "This is the beginning of the family oral history recording with (full name of the storyteller—spell the name)."

b) "I am the interviewer. My name is (state your name and spell it)."

c) "The date is (be sure to include the year)."

d) "This interview is taking place at (wherever you're located, e.g., the homeowner's address, city, state, or country)."

e) Provide a brief synopsis about the goal of the recordings. It may be as simple as "This recording with John Smith is for his life story and to obtain what family history he knows."

f) For any subsequent recordings, you need only say, "This is a continuation of the oral history interviews with (name)." Include the session date.

g) At the end of each interview session, state that it is the close of that session and whether it will be continued. When you reach the final session, state that it is the end of all recordings.

Tips for Topics

Don't carry a list of questions. Bring a list of topics. Phrase your topics in the following fashion: "Tell me about your home..." "Talk about your school days..." "That must have been a really interesting time to live here..." This forces the storyteller to tell a story and not just answer a question or say "yes" or "no." (*See Appendix A for more tips on how to prompt the storyteller.*)

Active Listening

In these oral history sessions, people may talk about the motivations behind life decisions. They might reveal their missed opportunities and what felt like their big successes. They often cry over the losses and disappointments. It is in an environment where you, the interviewer, need to be totally captivated and non-judgmental.

Your job as the interviewer is to be an active listener. For most of us, our inclination when in conversation is to be processing the information into how we relate to it and what we can say next on the subject. In the role of interviewer, you should take yourself out of the picture. Believe me, being a listener is a very active role—actually, a very intense activity. That's why you should limit the interview to about ninety minutes.

By being a rapt audience for the storyteller, you are conveying your enjoyment of their stories as well as your understanding, empathy, and compassion. This means looking at the storyteller frequently and not burying your head in your notes for the next topic. With your total focus, you are giving the storyteller the confidence that they're telling a worthy story.

Pay attention to the content of each story so you can follow up with questions to fill in the gaps. Visualize what the person is talking about so you can elicit more descriptive details. I urge you to refer to Appendix A for ideas on how you might nudge the storyteller to enhance their dialogue.

If the storyteller relates a very moving story, acknowledge it. For example, say, "I can see that was very difficult for you" or "I can see that making that decision took a great deal of courage."

Pats on the back are good. But be wary of too much of this so it doesn't seem contrived. And occasional laughter on your part in recognizing a joke is, of course, good, but too much loud laughter on your part can be a negative on the recording. A hearty smile can be sufficient.

Be wary of presuming you "get" the story being told. You may think you understand a situation, but sometimes what you assume is not what the narrator meant. This is where paraphrasing what you understood was said can be a very useful tool.

Being non-judgmental is critical. Whether you agree with someone's actions is irrelevant. You are there to allow them to tell their truth. You might prompt the storyteller to "educate" you so you can better understand their thinking behind an action. Be cautious about relating your own experiences as a way of expressing understanding or empathy. You have to feel this out because sometimes it works. Just keep in mind that the interview is not about you. Consider this: What if the storyteller thinks your story trumps theirs?

At some point, the storyteller may indicate he would like the recorder turned off to say something off the record. Ultimately, you have to honor their request to turn it off, but try not to do this. Explain that you can always edit things out later, but it'll be very difficult to have an off-the-record story told exactly the same way should they decide it can be included.

Pauses are a welcome thing. Very often these small breaks result in the storyteller chiming in with some additional thoughts. So try to get in the habit of pausing before posing the next topic.

Use these breaks yourself to go over the last story in your mind and make sure the basics have been included: who, what, where, when, why, and how—the reporter's standards.

Here are three great follow-up questions from retired personal historian Dan Curtis.

"What do you mean by that?"

"Can you tell me more?"

"Can you give me some examples?"

Ending

At the end of each session, you might ask the storyteller if there is anything they wanted to talk about that you didn't cover.

If you are going to conduct multiple sessions, listen to the previous recording before continuing into the next session. This will allow you to address anything that may not be audible and to bring some follow-up questions to fill in any gaps.

Having given you these directives, I want you to sit back and relax. Don't overthink the interview process. As long as you are engaged, fully listening, and have your focus on the storyteller, you will intuitively know what to ask, when to probe, when to sit back, and when to go on to the next topic.

After the Interviews

Do everything possible to safeguard these treasured recordings. Transfer them to your computer as soon as possible. Additionally, burn the recordings onto CDs or transfer them to a flash drive or portable hard drive. Put the recordings in two or more places in case of a natural disaster—fire, flood, earthquake, or computer malfunction. You may have a secure automated backup plan such as Carbonite[1] that satisfies that requirement. Some people keep their backup on hard drives in their safe deposit box or send copies to other family members as a precaution.

Now transcribe the recordings while they are still fresh in your mind.

---

[1] https://ww2.carbonite.com/

Chapter Three

Transcribing and Editing

ONE OF MY STUDENTS inherited about seventeen hours of audio recordings with family. She was surprised when I said they needed to be transcribed. It had never occurred to her that these audiocassette tapes were not going to last forever. Not only do cassette tapes deteriorate, as do CDs and DVDs, but you also have to consider that even the latest recording formats are going to become obsolete at some point.

For all of these reasons, it's very important to transcribe any recordings, video or audio, as soon as possible. You can transcribe the recordings yourself, a long and laborious process, or you can hire a professional transcription service provider.

If you're transcribing the interviews yourself, you'll likely remember what was said by the storyteller and thus can be sure the recordings are transcribed correctly. If you have someone else transcribe the audio for you, make sure to audit the transcript against the audio. It's quite possible the transcriptionist will hear a word incorrectly. When I came across an oral history recording of my father's at a local library, I listened to the audio against the transcript and, sure enough, there were a couple of errors. Since I was familiar with his speech patterns, it was easy for me to make the corrections.

There are helpful transcribing software programs available. Some free ones you can download are The Record Player,[2] Express Scribe,[3] and Transcriber Pro.[4] To locate others, do an online search for "free transcribing software." These programs allow you to open the digital audio recording on your computer and then play and pause the audio with your mouse or keyboard. Very nifty.

To locate a professional transcriber, you can search online for local providers or you can go to the Association of Personal Historians[5] site to find a transcriptionist. This is a good option because these transcriptionists are accustomed to working with oral histories specifically. I recently received an estimate from one of the transcribers listed at this personal historian site and the fee (year 2015) was $150 per recorded hour, assuming there are no problems with the clarity of the audio. Just so you have an idea, it takes approximately three to four hours to transcribe a one-hour interview. (*See Appendix B, page 73, for an example of a properly transcribed oral history.*)

What to Include and What to Delete

Always preserve a transcribed copy of the complete original recording with only minor editing. You may then edit the material even more for your family history book or use the manuscript to craft a narrative, but you still want to keep that full original transcript record. The following guidelines for acceptable minor editing are paraphrased from a long lost handout that was put

---

[2] http://www.fortherecord.com/

[3] http://www.nch.com.au/scribe/

[4] http://transcriber-pro.en.softonic.com/

[5] http://www.personalhistorians.org/

out at one time by the Oral History Center, The Bancroft Library, at the University of California in Berkeley, California.

- Reduce excessive static words such as "Well," "You know," "I think," "Okay," "Right," and "Of course." Retaining some of these expressions can provide the flavor of the vernacular speech pattern of the subject, but too many of them appearing over and over are distracting and thus detract from the subject matter.

- Edit for clarity, continuity, and elimination of repetitions.

- Omit the "ums," "ers," and "uhs" unless you see a definite need.

- Edit out emendations, additions, and approval by the interviewee.

- Add punctuation rather than allow run-on sentences that, when read, will make the material difficult to comprehend.

- If you are not sure whether something should stay or go, leave it in. Err on the side of including too much.

If there are dropped or missing words and you can recall what the storyteller said, type in the missing word. If you're not quite sure, fill in the word you suspect it is, but put brackets around the word. When the storyteller said a wrong word and it is clear what they meant to say, you can insert the right word with brackets around the word.

Refer back to your notes about the storyteller's non-verbal gestures or expressed emotions and bracket those next to the matching text, such as [laughing], [crying], [slams hand on the table in anger].

The Ethical Issues

Every family has secrets. And while some members of the family will want certain things revealed, others may be adamantly opposed.

Ask yourself if it is important that everyone knows this secret. If you honestly feel the information should not be lost, a suggestion for this type of dilemma is to write out the information, put it in an envelope, and on the outside of the envelope leave strict instructions as to when it can be opened. That could be a specific year or after a certain person in the family has died. Give the envelope to the family attorney or put it in a safe deposit box. If it's likely to be beyond your own lifetime, then make sure to reference this document in your will.

There is also an ethical and compassionate side to all this. It is a kindness to think of the descendants and what might be hurtful to them. Just because the storyteller said something doesn't necessarily mean it's appropriate to put it in print. It may in fact not be accurate, but rather one person's unique and possibly biased point of view. You may need to question the motive behind the telling of a particular story. A memoir shouldn't be an opportunity to rant about people in the family or tell tales that are cruel or mean-spirited.

One common situation is when anger from a divorce prevails. I've been working with a woman who is struggling with this in her memoir. Her children want to know her story, but she still has deeply hostile feelings toward her ex-husband, their father, and her question has become how to craft her memoir honestly without the anger dominating. In any judgment call, the family and descendants need to be the first consideration, in this case, her children.

I recall a client writing a memoir about an uncle who was a drunk and disrupted a family celebration one day; it did not make for a charming story. He ultimately decided not to include this story because the uncle's children and grandchildren would be reading this memoir and nothing was really gained by including this bit of ugly history.

In another instance, the storyteller did not want to talk about a medical issue. The younger members of the family were equally adamant that it needed to be known for the genetic implications.

Ultimately, it was agreed to honor the storyteller's wish. The younger members now have the option to make this medical situation known in their own memoirs.

The Memory Factor

Memory is a funny gal.[6] Family members are just naturally going to disagree about the truth of some of the stories. Inaccuracies are bound to occur. I always interview husbands and wives separately, and I just shake my head when I get a story about the same event because each person's version varies by degrees. These individuals certainly have a right to their memories. Your job as the writer of the memoir is to include the honest perspectives of people. If they disagree, so be it. I think it comes down to this: If you and I look outside from the same window and then sit down and write what we saw, there will invariably be differences. I will have noticed things you didn't and vice versa. And each of us may make mistakes, such as the actual color or shape of an object.

Once you have the transcript ready, send a copy to the storyteller for their verification of the facts and spellings. I always accompany the transcript with a letter in which I stress that the storyteller needs to recognize that the transcript is as he speaks and not as he would write the material, because there will be concern. It is natural for each of us to be critical when we see our words in print and concerned about how we will come across.

---

[6] "Gal:" Mnemosyne, the Greek goddess of memory and mother of the Muses by Zeus.

Part Two

Writing About Yourself

Chapter Four

Reasons to Write

MANY PEOPLE I EITHER KNOW or have worked with recently are deciding to write their own personal memoir. Many are determined from the outset to find a literary agent who will represent the book and sell it to a commercial publisher for a wide market. Others plan to self-publish the book, distribute it to family and friends, and maybe sell a few copies to anyone who is interested. Several intend to self-market their book in the hope of selling lots of copies, enough to have a major impact and even attract agents and publishers to take the book on for a commercial publication.

One reason for this surge in memoir writing is the population bulge of baby boomers who are sixty or over, the ripe age for memoir writing. Looking back, they realize they have had full and rich experiences, been part of events that rocked the world, had dealings with the rich and famous and/or people who made a major impact on the world, or traveled to parts of the world that will never again be as they were.

A person may want to use the memoir to take stock of their life journey, to figure out what happened, make sense of their lives, and tell their descendants about it. It can be a healing process, an act of self-analysis, and a means of passing down information, education, and inspiration to their children and grandchildren.

And let's not ignore the political and religious aspects to the personal memoir. Do you know someone who has powerful feelings about liberal or conservative politics, women's rights, gay marriages, and other hot-button topics? Someone who has a strong religious life that they feel a need to express? For these people, writing a memoir is motivated by a desire to present and persuade by writing a story about their lifetime of engagement, conflict, achievement, or frustration.

In contrast to these more intimate, personal motivations, many individuals write what's known as a "calling card." These are individuals in some kind of business who want people to hire them—consultants, life coaches, financial advisors—so their memoir is written with a deliberate focus on their success at whatever it is they're pitching. This is a perfectly legitimate type of memoir, often given away at workshops and training sessions, or sent to lists of potential clients. Writing such a memoir still requires many of the same techniques of researching, interviewing, and planning the structure for a compelling and convincing story.

And here's another reason why so many people are writing memoirs. Look at the best-seller lists. On a recent *New York Times* best-seller list, **_seven out of the top fifteen_** titles were memoirs, some by famous people, but just as many by people you never heard of before. It's amazing but true! People just love to read personal memoirs. It's a powerful reason to take a shot at it yourself.

Chapter Five

Making Your Story Come Alive

I urge you to pursue preserving your personal history to allow your children and grandchildren to know who you were as a child and what your hopes and dreams were.

—Oprah Winfrey

I'm not going to tell you writing is easy. Most people who decide to write their memoir are not professionals who've spent years learning the writing craft. They've never written a novel or even a non-fiction narrative that tells a story people want to read. Don't let that discourage you. I'm going to suggest several techniques and ideas that can get you started and gradually take you on a path towards successful storytelling.

Defining Your Core Journey

Okay. You're ready to get going. Think about what motivated you to make this decision. You just read some reasons people write a memoir—providing a legacy, figuring out and making meaning of what's happened in their life, beating the drum for something

they believe in, spreading the word about their professional services to get new clients. Whereas some of them may be partially
true for you, none is precisely on target for who you are and what
you want to do.

Talk to yourself. Talk to someone you love and trust. Tell
them what you care most about and what you don't want to leave
out of a memoir. Hone down to your core feeling: contentment
after a long struggle, regret and determination, pride, losses
you've overcome and how you did it.

Keep in mind one core universal truth about writing a memoir. *You have to be different at the end than you are at the
beginning*. The classic structure of any story is *transformation*.
Something has to happen. There has to be a problem, a situation
that challenged you. You have to fight, struggle, and work hard to
resolve it. At the end, you have to be transformed, come of age,
be older and wiser, made some progress, or realize something
about the original problem that brings closure. A place that at
least reaches a certain plateau of acceptance and a willingness to
keep going.

Keep Talking

Many folks use events in their lives to make a point when talking
to spouses, children, extended family, friends, and people they
work with. Maybe you do too.

If so, what you're doing is telling stories. Over time, these stories both remain the same and also change a little, but in important ways. You may change a word here and there, leave out
something while adding in something else. In short, you're inter-
nally editing these stories so they work better, make your point
clearer, cut to the chase. When you read what you've written out
loud and it sounds like you talking, you have succeeded.

This is exactly the kind of process that can lead to passages in
your memoir. So get out your keyboard and start writing. You
can also choose to record the stories and then transcribe them.
Here is a good example from someone who told this story many
times over the years and eventually put it in her memoir.

I went to a private school, Punaho, in Hawaii [1916]. To get there we got on the train to come to Honolulu. The train went along Pearl Harbor and then into Honolulu. Along the way, the train stopped for the children from the navy and the army posts. There were other posts not on the train route and those children lived in the dormitory at school.

When you got to the city, you jumped off the train and ran to catch the streetcar. Then you walked a quarter of a mile to your building. You had to catch the 5:15 train home or you had no way to get back. I used to wake up in the night from a recurring dream: I was running for the train and yelling for it to stop, stop . . . **STOP**!

My mother thought the train ride was too far for a first grader, so I waited until second grade to go to school. In place of first grade, my mother would say, "Go outside and look and listen, and you come back and tell me what you heard and what you saw."

There was a school on the plantation. All the plantation employees wanted their kids to go to school in the town. Since the children lived on the other side of the plantation from it, they had to walk—up and down, up and down—to get to school. It was a long walk. Years and years later, they finally did move the school because the hill was planted with sugarcane and they didn't want the kids to walk through the cane fields.

—Elizabeth Cooper Terwilliger, *The Honolulu Sugar Plantation*

Make a Plan

As I said in the section on writing another person's memoir, there are several ways you can tell any story. The most common approach is starting at the beginning, the chronological telling of one's life from childhood through adulthood. But as with writing another person's memoir, you can also start with a bang, at a key moment in your life, such as bringing home your first paycheck, being wounded in a war, losing a loved one, having a big success at work or being fired, having a terrible conflict with someone or reconciling—something dramatic with dialogue and action that both grabs the reader by the throat and also tells them something about the core feelings and transformational journey of the story they are about to read.

Once you've opened the book with that big bang, you can go back in time to the back story, to your birth, development, coming of age, and the events you select which relate to that core motivation and transformational journey.

Some authors like to write out a synopsis or summary. If you are artistically creative and can draw, you may want to make storyboards like they do when making a movie, with sketches representing moments in time and essential scenes. Many like an old-fashioned outline with fifteen or twenty chapters and three or four scenes in each chapter. Personally, I recommend writing out a prose paragraph (not bullets or short hand) of what happens in each scene. This allows you to print it out or put it up on the wall to see how it flows, whether there are any holes in the story or repetition or something is in the wrong place.

Another approach is to write your story as a series of vignettes or short stories. I rarely take this approach when interviewing someone, but many of my students find it easier to dig into this method. And they are oftentimes inspired when they think of these as short stories they might tell their grandchildren. Children love real stories about their parents and grandparents. And telling stories over and over again is what oral tradition is. Have you ever had a child say, "Tell me that story about . . . ."

After writing a number of these vignettes, you could then work in text bridges that would in some way link the stories so that there is a flow to the book. The goal here would be to craft a coherent sequential story, rather than random disconnected memories without focus or connectivity. Here is a preface written by someone who is right now writing his story as a series of events:

> I never wanted to write an autobiography nor is this intended to be one. I sought to pick out moments in my life when unusual things happened. Strange things, frightening episodes, happy moments, sad times—all the kinds of events that stand out in a person's memory. I tried to gather as many of these as I could recall and present them, in no particular order but grouped in roughly laid out chunks of my life. A

bit here, a piece there. If I had not done this, there will be nobody to remember these events once I am gone.

In addition to this, I want you to understand what a vastly different world I grew up in than the one in which we live today. (The year is 2012 as I write these words.) This was a world when times were hard. The Great Depression still held the country in its fearful grip. But it was also a primitive world in many ways, a world where milk was delivered in horse-drawn wagons, where icemen brought huge cubes of ice that kept cool the iceboxes that preceded the refrigerators of today, where trucks with iron-rimmed, wooden-spoked wheels clattered down cobblestone streets, where little girls wore pretty dresses and young boys wore knickers and funny caps. In short, it was nothing like the world we know today. In many ways, it was better than the present-day world; in other ways, it was worse. But good or bad, it deserves to be remembered. And that is one of the things I have tried to do on these pages.

The Craft of Writing

Whatever track you take you should look into the craft of writing. I use these following reminders when I am interviewing and going back to the storyteller to fill in gaps. I also look at these tips when I am writing for someone else.

Who, What, Why, When, Where, and How

In each of your stories and scenes, have you answered the five Ws and one H? Does the story tell you who it is about? What happened? When it took place? Where it took place? Why it happened? How it happened?

Narrative Voice

Narrative voice is what gives writing energy and authenticity. It animates the narrator and her story with a unique personality. It grabs your attention and keeps you turning the page.

The literary critic and memoirist Vivian Gornick describes the "truth-speaking" narrator of the story, an "I" with an attitude: "[The] narrator becomes a persona. Its tone of voice, its angle of vision, the rhythm of its sentences, what it selects to observe and what to ignore are chosen to serve the subject," she writes.

Here are some other points she makes. They may not all apply to you directly but at least some of them may resonate.

- Weed out the defensive, embarrassed, self-pitying, insecure, self-aggrandizing, or complaining.
- Weave a story of discovery, a journey from an unfinished self to a purposeful being, warts and all.
- Illuminate the small moments and telling details that illustrate the deeper meaning of what are otherwise random events.
- Welcome the dramatic buildup of uncertain outcomes and unresolved conflict. Readers can identify with this kind of reality, regardless of how the curtain falls.
- Think of your memoir as not a confession but a kind of self-investigation. Be honest about your own part in the situation, your "fear, whining, or self-hatred."

Examples

Giving examples draws the reader in. If someone managed money well, give a solid example that represents that trait. In one memoir, the storyteller said she went to a big town, so she wrote: "In 1904 I moved to town. Grafton was a pretty big town, being the county seat. There was a hospital. A feeble-minded institute. Stores and shops" (Lillian Cochrane Giles, *100 Years with Lily*).

Just saying there was a feeble-minded institute gives a good feel for the size of this town in North Dakota at the beginning of the twentieth century.

Description

If you can describe someone physically or tell us some character trait, you are putting the person on the page.

Lloyd Giles, another son who was away at the time of his brother's death, came home. He had a big laugh and was a good storyteller. No one could tell a story like Lloyd. He and his brother Charlie were as different as day and night. Where Charlie had been stout, Lloyd was lean. Lloyd was the wanderer. Mrs. Giles said, "I like all my children, but I love Lloyd." Because he was the wayward one. As our son George would say years later, "My dad and work are strangers." But I thought I could reform him. So on April 10, 1912, we were married by an Episcopal minister in Grand Forks, North Dakota.

—Lillian Cochrane Giles, *100 Years with Lily*

Anecdotes

Be sure to sprinkle in plenty of anecdotes. When interviewing, you achieve this by prompting, "Tell me about that town . . . Talk about that job . . ." etc. Use that same approach for yourself.

My dad joined the U. S. Navy in 1914. In 1919, he was sent to Vladivostok, Siberia. The Bolshevik Revolution was in progress and the Allied Forces were sent to there to keep the peace. The peacekeepers found themselves frozen in Siberia for almost two years.

It was there that my dad met a girl named Eda, but their romance didn't have a future. To my knowledge, Dad and Eda didn't keep in touch. I have a postcard addressed to her that Dad never mailed. But I am living proof that he never forgot her.

Whenever one of his sisters was expecting a baby, my dad would ask them to name it Eda if it was a girl. They all had boys. Then Dad had me, a little girl to name Eda.

For many years, my mother never knew that I was named for an old girlfriend. Then one evening my dad had a few beers and spilled the beans about the babe he met in Vladivostok. Mom was pretty mad. But then it had happened a long time before she and Dad met. So that is how I got the name, Eda.

—Eda Gebell, *Memories*

Dialogue

If your mother would scold you for your table manners, tell us what she would say. Even one sentence of dialogue livens things up.

I was about fifteen the day I almost died from cussing. I was doing my hair; it wasn't going the way I wanted it. Miss Drama Queen throws down her comb and says, "Well, shit!" My father was sitting at the kitchen table and said to me, "If you don't quit that god damn cussing I am going to knock the hell out of you." I started to laugh. I couldn't stop. Dad got up from his seat. He was coming to kill me, but I just laughed. Tears were rolling down my cheeks. I was thinking, *I'm gonna die.* But I was still laughing. Mom came into the kitchen. "Smitty," she said, "did you hear what you just said?" "Yes, goddamnit," and he started to swear at me again. Halfway through he stopped and then he started laughing. I lived to cuss another day.

—Eda Gebell, *Memories*

Feelings

Don't leave out feelings of anger, sadness, and joy. Tell us about that event that put tears in your eyes or rage in your heart.

At one point, I spanked Jane, who was very, very difficult. I gave her one licking and I said, "Oh, the hell with this." And Jane, who wasn't crying, then started crying. So while I didn't start crying I said, "No physical punishment." It doesn't work for one thing. And they're better off without it.

—Kristin Delaplane, ed., *Apple Henley: A Gentleman*

The Senses

A real showstopper in writing is slipping in the senses throughout. (Examples from Lillian Cochrane Giles, *100 Years with Lily*.)

- *Sound*: "Chickens crowing. Cow bells clanging. Mother never liked ducks, but she had geese. They were always yipping around."
- *Sight*: "She would shake ashes off her cigarettes behind the chairs so later she could see if I vacuumed there."
- *Touch*: "When it was cold, we had to wear our wool stocking caps. I hated mine because it would itch. As soon as I got past the barn, out of Mother's sight, I'd take it off and beat it with a stick."
- *Smell*: "I remember the raspberries and gooseberries. They were the sweetest-smelling plants."

- *Taste*: "We always had soup every day. Back then you could make a good soup because they gave you a good-sized beef bone. The kettle was on the back of the stove and we put in cut up carrots and celery and onion and bits of tomato. We'd add water to it every day and then use that good broth as the start for the day's soup."

Part Three

Preservation

Chapter Six

Organizing and Conservation

WHETHER YOU'RE WRITING someone else's memoir or your
own, you must preserve and protect all of the research, original
recordings, transcriptions, photographs, newspaper clips, maps,
and other memorabilia in a way that assures they'll be around
not only as you're writing but far into the future for your
descendants. For one, they may want to see how you drew your
conclusions and what resources you had available. Two, they may
find they want to do a different project and can make use of these
materials in a different way.

Back up your computer files in two or three different places
as well as any writings or audio or video you created and
research records you found and copied. This way you have safe-
guarded your treasures and hard work in case of a computer
crash or a natural disaster—flood, earthquake, or fire. Think of
getting these copies to other family members or storing them in
a safe deposit box or both.

Getting Organized

Develop a set of working folders in your computer and a file box. Even though I scan most of my materials, I always find use for a file box. And if you don't use a computer extensively, then your working folders will organized in a file box. (*See Appendix C, page 75, for an example of a naming system for folders and subfolders.*)

Protecting Your Materials

Invest in some archival supplies. Having your items just stuffed into cardboard or plastic boxes puts them at risk to fade or otherwise deteriorate. Most office supply stores carry some archival supplies, particularly archival sleeves. You can also purchase them online, which is what I do. Among the leading companies in this field are Gaylord Archival,[7] Light Impressions,[8] and Print File.[9] Gaylord Archival has a starter kit, "My Family History Kit." My favorite go-to item is the archival sleeve. At Gaylord it's the "3 or 4 mil Archival Polyester Envelopes with Edge Seal." I use these handy encasements for practically everything: photographs, letters, documents, and small booklets.

When purchasing your supplies, consider if you have any items that are bigger than a regular banker's file box. They do have archival boxes that are oversized, so you may want to invest in one or more if you have oversized artifacts or delicate objects, such as christening gowns. Make sure you layer any textiles with archival tissue paper.

---

[7] http://www.gaylord.com/
[8] http://www.lightimpressionsdirect.com/
[9] http://www.printfile.com

Some Archival Supplies

All images on this page are courtesy of Gaylord.com. Used by permission.

Archival boxes

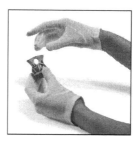

White cotton gloves are good when handling very old paper material and textiles. Hands have oils that can cause damage.

Top-loading sheet protectors

Preserving Photographs

Many people don't organize their print photographs very carefully, often just tossing them in a shoebox or maybe keeping them in the original photo processor's envelope. As a result, when those pictures are handed down, they can't always be easily identified and are also subject to deterioration.

First step: Gather your collection together. If you have albums that have been passed down and you can't identify half the people, consider dismantling the album and saving only the relevant photos. My grandmother had one of those albums with black heavy paper to which the photos were glued. Do not attempt to remove the photo from the backing. Cut out the photo with its backing from the album.

Now, go through your pictures to identify them. Show the photographs to your relatives and see what they can tell you about them. Put numbers on the back of a photo with a grease pencil made especially for that purpose and make a separate list identifying each shot. Never ever use a pen on the back of a photograph as it can (and probably will) leak through to the front and never ever write on the front of it. Sometimes you cannot write on the back because of the paper used, such as Polaroid photos. In that case, stick a post-it note on the back as a temporary solution.

Next, scan each photograph. Scanning at 300 dpi is just fine. Decide a system for naming your scanned files. Don't try to make the name descriptive of the photograph. I usually have my photographs separated into categories. That may be a particular person, a branch of the family, a particular trip, and so on. I then name the photos with the category name and numbers. For instance: Delaplane ancestors-1, Delaplane ancestors-2, Delaplane ancestors-3, etc.

Just a note: Color print photographs have a relatively brief lifespan. They'll fade. That is yet another nudge as to why you should scan your photos as soon as possible. And you might consider having quality black and white photographs taken at your next big event, such as a wedding, because black and white photographs will last if stored properly.

To create a descriptive record of photographs, I use my computer to place each photo on a single page with a caption and then go on to the next page in my document to add the next captioned photo. My captions tell as much as I know about the photo: names of the people, any objects that may have family interest, and the computer file name of the digitized photograph. (*See Appendix C, page 76, on how to create a descriptive record and to see an example.*)

As I scan each photograph, I place the original in an archival sleeve protector and then layer it into an archival box. Once I have the box full, I print out my descriptive record document, placing it on the very top. Now whenever anyone opens that file box, they can see exactly what is inside with that descriptive record in place. Naturally, I keep this descriptive record in my computer along with the digitized photographs. I have all my scanned photos of my ancestors in a folder called Delaplane Ancestors Photos, and the descriptive record document is in the same folder.

Protecting Your Papers

Family memorabilia, such as news clippings and letters, are common items found in the family shoebox. They may be folded, glued, stapled, or paper clipped. Rather than using paperclips, my grandmother used straight pins from her sewing basket. Well, metal of any kind is a disaster. You have probably seen rust on paper from paperclips. Your goal is to release each item from bondage and rehouse it in a safe environment.

It's fairly easy to get rid of creases or folds on paper. This process must not be used on photographs. Put distilled water in the bottom of a steamer. Heat the water and remove from heat source. Put the object in the vented steamer and allow to rest overnight. If you don't have a steamer, use this idea to create your own setup with a pan of water, some kind of platform above the water, and aluminum foil as your vented top.

Ungluing paper goods from a backing is also pretty straight-forward. Again, this process must not be used on photographs. Moisten a cotton ball with distilled water and gently pat the paper where the glue is. You do not want the paper soaking wet. Place plastic wrap over the object and allow to rest overnight. In the morning, release the paper by starting at the corners using a light touch with a spatula.

Once your item is ready, scan it as you did your photographs and create a descriptive record. Put the original items in the protective sleeves and layer in an archival box with the descriptive record on top.

In organizing your collection, if you must use glue for any of your paper goods (excluding photographs), use white glue. If it says "non acidic" or "acid free," that is exactly what you want. If you must use paperclips, use plastic coated ones.

Audio and Video Recordings

Make sure you do three things:

1) As mentioned before, store copies in several family households.

2) Run your audio or video at least once a year. This practice assures that the wheels are still running.

3) Keep migrating your audio and video to the latest technologies. This applies to any digital files you have, including text files. We pretty much know that in twenty years technology will have zoomed beyond DVDs. We also know in time these items will not last and because in the future, even if they do last, no one will be able to access them without a great deal of hassle. If you have any "ancient" recordings, such as cassette tapes or VHS tapes, or slides, get them migrated now. There are several companies you can find online that provide this service.

Storage

Store your archival boxes in a stable environment that is out of
the sun. A closet floor is usually ideal. A dry basement could be
good. Avoid places where the humidity is very low or over fifty
percent.

Artifacts

Start identifying the family heirlooms, the objects that have been
passed down. I recommend including information in an appendix at the end of your memoir. Just as with your photographs and
paper ephemera, photograph each heirloom and create a
descriptive record. In your caption information, give all the
details about the item such as the maker, what the object is made
of, dimensions, its history and importance, and its current condi-
tion. State who currently has the item and who is set to inherit it.
(*See example of an artifact with caption in Appendix C, page 78.*)

Part Four

Finding and Documenting Your Ancestors

Chapter Seven

Genealogy

GATHER ALL THE FAMILY HISTORY material you already have. I suggest filling out a paper form family tree before entering anything in a computer or online. Do an online search to find paper forms at no cost. (*See Appendix D, page 79, for an example of a free blank Family Tree form.*)

Once you are satisfied your paper forms are filled out to the best of your knowledge, you are ready to enter the information into a computer family tree. Again, do an online search for "top ten genealogy software" to compare programs, ratings, and features. RootsMagic Essentials[10] is a decent free program; it's a good starting point to get your feet wet. Or, instead of installing a program, you can put your information online at sites such as Geni,[11] or My Heritage.[12]

---

[10] http://www.rootsmagic.com/essentials/

[11] http://www.geni.com/

[12] https://www.myheritage.com/

If you do not use a computer program, then stick to the paper form. Next you will be researching your genealogy.

The Treasure Hunt

Certainly the first places to go are the major Internet sites: Ancestry.com or FamilySearch.org. Ancestry is a fee-based website, although they do have a free option with limited features. Family Search is a free website. They have both been making great strides in adding not only data but also providing newbie genealogists with great how-to tips. If you're not comfortable conducting these searches at first, join a genealogy club or society so people can assist you. At first, limit your search to your direct ancestors and work one branch at a time.

A word of caution: When you do these searches, you'll get leads to other people's family trees. Be sure their information came from solid sources such as birth, marriage, and death records. These are known as primary sources. And whenever you enter some information in your tree, make a note as to your source for that data.

Conduct your online searches based on what you know. I know my great-great grandfather's name was Jew D. Delaplane, so I would enter his name in the search section. Let us assume the only thing I know is his name. On the next page, you can see all the "hits" I got with just that information at Ancestry. I can now choose one of these records to see if this is my ancestor. I pulled up the census record of 1860, and I know this is my kin.

📷 Illinois, Wills and Probate Records, 1772-1999 WILLS, PROBATES, LAND, TAX & CRIMINAL View Image	NAME: Jew Delaplane DEATH: Abt 1906 - Illinois, USA CIVIL: Apr 1906 - Cook, Illinois, USA
📄 1880 United States Federal Census CENSUS & VOTER LISTS View Image	NAME: Jew Delaplane BIRTH: abt 1853 - Ohio RESIDENCE: 1880 - Lathrop, Clinton, Missouri
📄 Cook County, Illinois, Deaths Index, 1878-1922 BIRTH, MARRIAGE & DEATH	NAME: Jew D Delaplane BIRTH: abt 1852 DEATH: 9 Mar 1906 - Cook, Illinois, United States OTHER: United States
📄 U.S. City Directories, 1822-1989 SCHOOLS, DIRECTORIES & CHURCH HISTORIES View Image	NAME: Jew Delaplane RESIDENCE: 1871 - Berrien, Michigan, USA
📄 U.S., Civil War Pension Index: General Index to Pension Files, 1861-1934 MILITARY View Image	NAME: Jew Delaplane
📄 1860 United States Federal Census CENSUS & VOTER LISTS View Image	NAME: Jew Delaplane BIRTH: abt 1852 - Ohio RESIDENCE: Oronoko, Berrien, Michigan
📄 U.S., Find A Grave Index, 1600s-Current BIRTH, MARRIAGE & DEATH	NAME: Jew D Delaplane BIRTH: 1852 - Ohio, USA DEATH: 9 Mar 1906 - Chicago, Cook County, Illinois, USA
📄 U.S. Army, Register of Enlistments, 1798-1914 MILITARY View Image	NAME: Jew Delaplane BIRTH: abt 1851 - Ohio, United States MILITARY: 30 Jul 1873

Chart courtesy of Ancestry.com

When you obtain a census record, be sure to look at the whole page and even the page before and the page after. Case in point: I was looking for the mother of one of my clients, but she did not show up in the family home on the census. I found her listed in a neighbor's household. Likely she was visiting there that day and the enumerator simply lumped her in. It is not a perfect system.

Find a Grave[13] is a fabulous website for locating your ancestors' gravestones. You can search for your ancestor's name and there may already be a record, what they call "memorials." If not, contact the cemetery to get the specific gravesite location and create a "memorial" at Find a Grave. Then put in a request for a photograph. Ask them to transcribe all the information that appears on the gravestone and to shoot the grave head-on rather than shooting down. I had a volunteer take one photo and they did not include the inscription information, which was fairly extensive. In another instance, the person took a photo shooting down. A number of months later I was able to visit the cemetery. The stone had slipped down in the dirt over the years. When I tilted it up to see the rest of the inscription, I was able to pinpoint the exact town the person was from in Ireland. So be forewarned and be specific in your request.

For immigration searches try Ellis Island, and for immigrant ship manifests try One-Step Webpages, Immigrant Ships Transcribers Guild, and Olive Tree Genealogy.

Military records are an important source of information, too. A site like Ancestry.com has records specific to military records, as well as probate records and wills.

---

[13] http://www.findagrave.com/

[14] http://www.stevemorse.org/

[15] http://www.immigrantships.net/

[16] http://www.olivetreegenealogy.com/index.shtml

Digging Deeper

Newspapers can lead you to information about births, marriages, and deaths. Newspaper obits will give you names of family members, a very helpful jumping-off point.

Try different spellings of the name. From about 1880 through the mid-1920s, America experienced an immigration boom, "the Great Wave." During this time, names were often shortened or Americanized. In searching for a person named "Leonardo," I found the first name "Ontario" attached to one of his census records. I did a search with just the first name "Ontario." Bingo. I pulled up my Leonardo. In researching another family, I found that the family's last name had been changed by an employer. To the present day, the family has been known by the last name this employer pulled out of the air, but the ancestors had to be researched under the original name.

Another family emigrated from Ireland during the Potato Famine. They changed the ages for the whole family, making everyone five years younger than was recorded with their Irish church records. One supposition is that it ensured that all of the children made it through immigration, as minors were allowed to enter with their mother as long as they were healthy. The eldest was actually eighteen, so taking off the five years made her a minor, but she would have looked odd compared with her siblings, so the family as a whole simply knocked five years off everybody's ages, and those remained their official ages for the rest of their lives.

Other sources of information are state census records, maps, and land records. Do not assume that all records are now posted on the Internet. Here is where church records can be a font of information.

Contact the historical societies or libraries in the towns that figure in your family's history. They may have information about your family. I had a client whose family had immigrated to a small town in Wisconsin. Upon contacting the town's historical society, I was able to get a small book they had put out on the history of the town, which included a photo of the company housing. That was a stroke of luck as her ancestor had lived in the company housing. As a rule, historical societies operate with volunteers and they almost always go out of their way to be helpful. They may charge a small fee for copies they send you, but whether they charge a fee or not, please consider a small donation.

Lastly, there is a site Random Acts of Genealogical Kindness. You can access their website or hook up at Facebook.[17] This is a group of volunteers who will help you with records you are having trouble locating or are in a town other than where you are.

Finding the Descendants

Reach out to people who share your ancestry. You never know what photographs or family memorabilia have been passed down to them. By doing this kind of research, I was able to obtain photos of my client's great grandfather as a young man. I found the descendant's name by going to newspaper obits, and then I used the online white pages to find this distant cousin. Online genealogy sites such as Ancestry can be useful here, too. There may be descendants who have posted family trees and you can connect with them to share information.

I have also had good fortune by setting up family group pages on Facebook. My family found an ancestor's powder horn from Revolutionary War days with our page.

Cataloging Your Source Documents

I recommend cataloging your source documents—census records; birth, death, and marriage certificates; deeds; wills; and so on—in the same manner as I catalog my photographs and memorabilia. Scan the record. Determine a system for naming your images. Mine is "date, type of source, and name of person." The 1860 census I found for Jew Delaplane I named "1860–US Census–Jew Delaplane."

---

[17] https://www.facebook.com/groups/33868082803/

I printed out the census, put it in an archival sleeve, and put it in an archival box. I started my descriptive record of sources. These captions are to isolate all the information in the document about your ancestor(s) so you have a ready record. Make note of any corrections to the source document in the caption.

As an example: "CORRECTION: The birth date is incorrect in this census record. The actual birth date was _____." When I put my book together, I will put these descriptive records in an appendix with a table of contents. (*See Appendix D, pp. 80-81, for examples of captioned primary sources.*)

Writing the Family History

View writing about your ancestors as presenting the information in sections: storytelling sections and a genealogy section. The problem with many family histories is that they are simply not reader friendly. Including census records and detailed mentions of property records loses the storytelling flavor. I rarely refer to the source records. Rather than writing, "In the 1880 census . . ." I will simply write, "In 1880 . . . ."

As with memoir writing, you want to start the story of the ancestral branch with some dramatic event, such as the beginning of this story that was written by my ancestors. Please allow that they didn't know about political correctness and it was surely also exaggerated with the telling over the years. Yet, all descendants of this family have some version of this story.

Western Kentucky—"The Dark and Bloody Ground"—bordering the Ohio River was held by the Indians as a great hunting park, and was supposed to be friendly to the "pale face." On the afternoon of October 23, 1762, two large hunting parties, who had secured all the game needed for their winter supply, started for their respective homes. A chief was along with each party, and "for pure Indian meanness" they took Ben Hill and his son prisoners and confiscated their horses and outfit. The chief living up the river got the boy, one half of the outfit, and one horse, while the chief living down the river got the old man, one horse, and the other half of the outfit. The Indians had a great feast that night and wound up with a war dance. They were to start next morning for their respective homes.

After you write your dramatic story, go back to the back-story and write about your ancestors chronologically. Such as this beginning:

> Tradition tells us that a Benjamin Hill of Scotch-Irish descent, a man of education and substance and a solider or officer in the French and Indian War, left the Old Dominion, Virginia, in 1762 and took up a claim in what is now West Virginia, near the Monongahela River.
>
> —Laurence Lee Hill,
> *Hardy Hill of Kentucky: His Life and Descendants*

You may well have some big stories that seem to interrupt the narrative flow. I have a story written by one of my ancestors about his experiences during the Revolutionary War. While I say in the family history storyline he was in the war and include a couple of sentences about that, I created a section in the book named "Direct Ancestral Stories" that follows this family history narrative and dropped the full details of my big stories there. Likewise, I have a couple of great stories about not-direct ancestors, so I added a section called "Not-Direct Ancestors" to present those lip-smacking stories.

How to Write Your Genealogy

Follow the sections about the family history with a written genealogy. This is not the same as a family narrative because it is not told in story form. It gives the reader a concise way for people to follow the family tree. And, likely not everything in this layout will have been mentioned in your narrative. (*See Appendix D, page 82, for an example of this.*)

Part Five

Design, Production, and Marketing

Chapter Eight

Graphics

YOU HAVE THE OPPORTUNITY to place graphic elements throughout your book that will enhance and help tell the stories. Among these graphics are photographs, various views of the family tree, news clippings, maps, timelines, family recipes, and signatures. Play with your graphics. They are an enjoyable part of piecing a book together.

Family Trees

You can add a family tree graphic created from your family tree software program, or you can insert a large family tree that people can unfold. This family tree graphic gives the reader yet another way of understanding the ancestral lines. I encourage you to also add family tree graphics throughout the book as is appropriate to make the story easier for the reader to follow. With a computer program you create specialized views of the relationships, which go a long way in helping the reader identify the family lineage. (*See Appendix E, pp. 85–86, for examples of family tree graphics.*)

Placing Photos in Your Book

Determining which photographs to include in your book can be challenging. Don't get me wrong, I like photographs; but I also think you need to avoid overdoing it. Think of your descendants. Don't bore them. Make this an exciting collection.

Weed out photos that are redundant. You don't need five pictures of Katie's fifth birthday party. The thought process I follow is this: Does the photograph match and enhance the story? The memoir/family history is not meant to be a photo album. If you want to showcase more photos, I suggest you create a companion book or add more photos in the appendix.

A popular style today in placing photos is what is referred to as "word wrap." You may have seen this where the text wraps around the photo. It can be very effective, but I like to put the photos in blocks of pages throughout. This is the style used in older, traditional books. In having the photographs separate from the text, the reader will place more focus on them, and you can make each photograph as large as is appropriate within the dimensions of the book. Remember, this may be the only photograph of the great-grandfather the reader will ever have.

If you do decide to place photos or graphics on pages with text, make sure to surround them with ample white space. These graphics should stand out, holding the reader's attention.

Historical Backgrounds

Including short histories of the circumstances, like a pandemic, or about the region where the memoir takes place, can be a nice graphic detail. Set the text in a textbox or use a distinctive font. Put this type of graphic at the very beginning as a lead in, at the end as a fade out, or in an appendix.

For example, if your family originated in Scotland, you could write a short history about the family's clan and the area where the clan members lived. Dress this up with period drawings, photographs, and maps if you want.

Brief histories about the places of importance in the storyline, such as the town where a parent grew up or where the original settlers immigrated, can be helpful in creating an atmosphere of time and place. (*See Appendix E, page 87, for an example of a city history.*)

Maps

Maps are one of the best additions to any story. Nowadays you can easily insert arrows to highlight locations or insert names of streets that no longer exist.

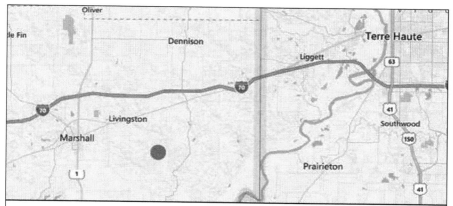

Map data © 2015 Google

1853 Grave of Isaac Hill

[Dec 22, 1784–Feb 11, 1853]

A view of the ancestor's grave location in Illinois near the Indiana border. Isaac Hill is buried in a family graveyard that was on his farm on Big Creek outside of Marshall, Illinois. The circle on the map indicates the location.

Timelines

Timelines, while a graphic element, are usually placed in the appendix. For every memoir and ancestral narrative, present timelines. It gives the reader yet another way to envision the story as well as being a quick reference guide. (*See Appendix E, pages 88–90, for some timeline examples.*)

Chapter Nine

Making the Book

SOMETIMES THE MOST DIFFICULT step in preparing a memoir is putting the baby to bed. To say the book is done. No more editing. No more drafts. No more added information. Time to make this a book!

The Cover Design

You may have written your memoir as a book to sell. If so, create a book with a telling cover. The cover tells the world the title and the author, and what the book is about—that it is a *memoir*. It may also quote on the front or back who else read and enjoyed the book with endorsements, testimonials, and marketing blurbs.

Your book cover should also be a powerful graphic design that catches the browser's eye, whether it's a small version on Amazon or in the window of a retail bookstore.

When you're self-publishing, there are generic templates offered from vendors like CreateSpace (an Amazon company).[18]

---

[18] https://www.createspace.com/

Or, if you want to try for something better, something more original, and something that is more likely to sell books, you can hire
the same professional cover designers traditional publishers use.
This requires a greater financial investment—between $3,000
and $5,000—but you can also find designers who will do it for
between $300 and $500. Often, a cover designer may be able to
either sub-contract the interior page design of the book or do it
themselves—an additional $1,000 to $2,000. My local copy place,
AlphaGraphics, does book designs. They advertise their company
as a "full-service print shop," so that would be another type of
company to look into. There are family history book design spe-
cialists, too. You could do an online search or search for them at
the Association of Personal Historians site. Since everything is
done with file transfers, you don't have to be located in the same
town.

Of course, you can opt to do it all yourself using a word-
processing program such as Microsoft Word or Apple's Pages.
But bear in mind these programs are not book design programs,
so there are a number of common book elements you cannot
produce easily, such as running heads and good drop caps. If you
want to use a design quality software, look to Adobe InDesign or
Microsoft Publisher.

Whether you hire someone or do it yourself, be sure to select
fonts that are easy on the eye. Though you may be tempted, we
advise you to avoid fancy, ornamental fonts. Serif fonts, such as
Times New Roman, Garamond, Palatino, or Georgia are best for
the main body of text. Headings and subheadings can be set in
sans-serif fonts, such as Helvetica, Arial, or Calibri to set them
apart from the body text and give your book design some flare.

Binding
If you're planning a limited edition of your memoir just for family
and friends, you can search online for bookbinders who offer a
range of bindings from leather with gold stamping to fine cloth
binding.

If your plan includes both producing a number of books for an extended list of give-aways to a large group of family, friends, fellow workers, and—perhaps—the general market at large, then you can either print-on-demand through vendors like Amazon's CreateSpace or Lightning Source,[19] or you can go directly to a larger printing company and order a few thousand copies. It used to be that offset printing was advised for this, but today high-quality digital printing is so good that I advise you look into that.

E-books, of course, don't have any binding, but they still need a cover and interior page design.

Copyright

Copyright is automatic with anything created by you. You may formally copyright a book by writing "Copyright ©" followed by the year of publication in the book and your name on the inside left-hand page after the title page.

If you do want to register a formal and official copyright to your work, you may do so through the Copyright Office, Library of Congress, in Washington, DC. You can also apply online at *www.copyright.gov*.

The Book in Hand

You are holding your book. Congratulations! Are you ready for your book party? What a terrific excuse to hold a family reunion. And what a special gift for the family.

There are several products that might ensue from your book. This might prompt someone in the family to put together a yearly newsletter. Another possible offshoot is for someone in your family who is tech savvy to set up a website where family tree information can be updated and new photos uploaded. With my different family tree branches as Facebook groups, all the family members from that branch can interact, ask questions, and post family photographs or family news. It is quite fun and serves to

---

[19] https://www.lightningsource.com/

bring new family members into the mix, thus seeing the interest pass down through the generations.

If you haven't already made some kind of informal family video for YouTube, then that is another project that someone could take up: producing a documentary showing the family beginnings to the current day.

Have you considered donating this book to an appropriate archive, such as the local historical society in the town where you or the storyteller grew up or where the ancestors lived? If you feel some of the material in the book is not suitable for public consumption, then maybe consider just donating the sections that might be of historical interest to the depository. The pages are enough. They don't need an entire book.

Now as I bid you *adieu*, I wish you all the best in your endeavor and hope that my bit of knowledge will be that helpful guidance and encouragement you need as you proceed to leave your mark, capture your stories, and hand down the family legacy.

There have been great societies that did not use the wheel, but there have no societies that did not tell stories.

—Ursula K. LeGuin

Part Six

Appendixes

Appendix A

Refer back to Chapters One and Two

Evoking Important Memories (*see page 5*)

Home Life: Family members. Family talents. Family physical characteristics. Daily life and routines. Meals. Food preservations practices (cellars, ice blocks, etc.) Chores. Rules. House décor. Play. Activities. Vacations. Celebrations. Music. Reading. Pets. Cars. Reunions. Moves. Affection. Tidiness of home. Holidays.

Childhood: Appearance. Hairstyle. Dress. Friends. Mentors. Successes. Failures. Favorite activities. Lunch foods. Discipline. Allowance. Sports. Fads. Games.

Education: Schools. Scholastic aptitude. Activities. Awards. Thoughts on education. Social life. Training. Continuing education.

Money: Family circumstances. Income level. How income affected values, priorities, social life, and opportunities. Cost of food, clothes, furniture, etc

Military: Branch of service. Opportunity. Experiences. How this affected person's life direction.

Work: Jobs. Responsibilities. Work environments. Commute. Career. Goals. Attitude about work. Mentors and co-workers. Accomplishments. Thoughts about industry or profession.

Community: Organizations. Clubs. Volunteer activities.

Politics: Political activities in school. Political activities as a citizen. Voting habits and choices.

Religion: Family practices. Personal beliefs. How your spiritual practices or lack of affected your life.

Health: Medical history. Accidents. Childhood illnesses. Health practices. Chronic problems. General attitude about health.

Friendships: Social life. School friends. Church friends. Work friends. Lifelong friends. Qualities in a friend.

Pets: First pets (birds, gerbels, puppies, kittens). Growing up with animals. Their illness and death. Getting animals as an adult, as a parent.

Diet/Exercise: Nutritional practices. Food likes and dislikes. Exercise.

Sexuality: First awakenings. Puberty. Learning about sex. Teen years. Attitude about sex. Identifying with role models.

Romance: Puppy love. Early dating. Courtship. What you learned about love.

Marriage: Making the decision. Proposal. Wedding. Honeymoon. Division of chores. Joys and sorrows. Disagreements. Compromises. Thoughts on marriage.

Children: Births. Parenting methods. Dreams and hopes for children. Thoughts about each child.

Divorce: Reasons. Amicable or not. Finances. Custody. How family members were affected. Current status and understanding.

Retirement: Forced through corporate attrition or personal choice. Wishing you could stay on. Difficult transition. Living at home with or without partner/ spouse. Developing new structure and activities. Thoughts about aging.

Tips for Topics (*see page 13*)

How to Prompt a Storyteller

Tell me about your mother . . .

Describe your childhood home . . .

I would be interested in hearing about your hometown . . .

I am curious about a typical day in your childhood . . .

Describe your family's social position . . .

Talk about your early dreams . . .

Educate me about your opportunities . . .

I am curious about your expectations in life . . .

I would be interested in hearing about your challenges . . .

Detail your successes . . .

So, briefly, you start each topic with a phrase such as:

Describe . . .

Tell me about . . .

I would be interested in hearing about . . .

I am curious about . . .

That must have been an interesting time . . .

How would you advise someone in a similar situation . . .

Educate me about . . .

Talk about . . .

Detail . . .

Example of a Memoir

John Vasquez

It was 1935 and our family was living in a big cutting shed. We used to make our own shower: take some fruit trays, stand them up and then get a garden hose. Put some holes in a tin can over the hose and that was our shower.

My parents were both born in Mexico. They entered the United State in 1920 at Laredo, Texas. After my dad completed a year working in Texas for the railroad, they moved to Bosworth, Mis-souri. In 1923, they moved to Sheridan, Wyoming. And in 1926, the move was to Deadwood, South Dakota. This was all railroad work. Then from 1926 to 1935 they lived in Nebraska where as a family we worked in sugar beets. That was field work.

Then in the last of '35 when I was five years old we left Nebraska for Los Angeles. That was his big dream—to come to California. My parents had some friends they had worked with in a sugar factory who had moved to Knights Landing, California, so from Los Angeles we moved to Knights Landing. But my dad couldn't put the family to work there because it was the season of school.

Then he found out in Vacaville (the next town) there was a chance put the whole family to work picking prunes. [These were prune plum trees, so referred to as "prunes" by the farmers.] The fruit is in the summertime when the kids were on their vacation. My father would shake the prunes off the tree. They had poles. The poles had like a hook on them and you shake the limbs. Then whatever prunes were left, you turn the pole around and hit them with the other end, the end without the hook. We kids picked the prunes off the ground, put them in a bucket and then put them in a box. Then the farmer would come and pick up the boxes

When we came to Vacaville, the first place we ended up was where the Medical Facility is today. They didn't really have facilities for us to live there, so we lived in the cutting shed. It was a lot of fun for me. It was just like a big barn. We had some of those army cots and some of us just slept on the floor on a mat-tress. My mother had a kerosene stove and some of the time they had a wooden stove outside. She cooked chili, rice, beans, tortillas, potatoes, fideo. We only lived there one prune season.

—Oral history for Vacaville Museum exhibit and book:
Solano's Gold: The People and Their Orchards

Appendix B

Refer to Chapter Three

Oral History Transcription

Example of a properly transcribed oral history. This is not the only way to format a transcript, but this style is easy to read.

Interview with Stanton Delaplane
Interviewer: Carl Mosher
October 14, 1978

Session One
(Tape 1, Side A) (This was from the days of cassette tapes.)

Carl Mosher: For the past quarter-century or so, give or take a few years, I've improved my temper and my breakfast in the morning by reading a daily column entitled "Postcard" by Stanton Delaplane. These Postcards are notable for their humor, their information, their anecdotes, and a general warmth that I've always admired and found very comforting. How do you do it?

Stanton Delaplane: Well, you sit down in the morning at about nine o'clock. This is the way I do it. Other guys may do it differently, but I don't think they do it much differently. I get up and make coffee, and I sit down. This is a very important thing—to sit down in front of the typewriter. Don't sit down in another corner because if you do you'll never hit the typewriter. Then I promise myself I'll just write one paragraph, because I really don't want to do this. After one paragraph, it takes me about forty-five minutes, and I've got a column away. It's not quite that easy, but I think that will give you the idea. Everybody has a different type of column, mine happens to be sort of an entertaining column. I have discovered that it's something like a comic strip in a way. People don't want you to change their picture of you. They don't want me to do politics, for instance. I don't make any political statements, and I don't come out for one thing or another. Herb Caen does. That's his way of doing it. Maybe some guy in New York does an entirely different thing—like Earl Wilson, who hammers on the show business thing; "Who's at the Mocambo" or whatever the big club is at this time. We all have our thing. Herb Caen would die doing what I'm doing. So would Earl Wilson.

Mosher: I know one of the techniques you use is delightful family tidbits and talk, which everyone enjoys, and, of course can all identify with, all of us who've had families.

Delaplane: That's true. Everyone identifies with it because these things happen to all of us. I think people are surprised that it happens to somebody else the same way it happens to them. They think their experience with children is unusual—that kids can do these terrible things to you and be so blasé about it. They don't think it could happen to anybody else. Then they read it in the column and say, "Gee, it happens to him, too." It has kind of a good value because it lets off a little steam for the guy or the woman who reads it. She says, "Well, it's not just me with my children."

Appendix C

Refer to Chapter Six

Getting Organized

An example of a naming system for folders and subfolders (*see page 40*).

- ▲ Smith Family Book
  - Appendicies
  - Catchall file
  - Family documents
  - Family profiles
  - ▲ Genealogy
    - Ancestral stories
    - Family trees
    - Souce documents
  - Graphics
  - Heirlooms
  - ▲ Memoirs
    - Chapters
    - Oral history recordings
    - Oral history transcripts
    - Reflections
  - To do tasks

Note that under the Genealogy folder there are three subfolders. One contains the story development of the ancestors, another the family tree software results, and the third holds the source documents, such as census records and birth records, found during the research process. The Memoirs folder also has subfolders that are self-explanatory.

About the Graphics folder. Undoubtedly, you have some paper documents such as news clipping and letters. I suggest you scan each document and put the scanned files in your Graphics folder, and, as I said, retain the original copies in your archival box.

I also recommend an active To Do Tasks folder. Set up a system for noting the tasks you need to get to. It may be that you want to look up the history of your town or make a copy of a particular photograph or call a brother so he can send you a newspaper clipping. There are going to be a number of these types of tasks as you go along, so keeping track of your progress is essential.

The Catchall folder is for that material or ideas for which you have not yet found a home. It might be the notation of a story you will want to include. It could be a nod to a family reunion. Perhaps a quote you may want to use somewhere.

Preserving Photographs (*see page 42*)

This is an example of setting up your photos with captions.

I use Microsoft Word to create my descriptive record, so I will include those directions here. Insert a single column table. Place the scanned image into the table. If you do not put the image in a table, it will not stay put on the page. Use the tab key to create a new row in your table, which is for your caption. If the photo is too large to have the photo and caption on the same page, use your mouse at the corners of the picture to reduce it in size until both photo and caption reside on one page.

See the resulting picture and caption on the facing page.

Helen Miriam Kleinert

Taken above Baker Beach in the Presidio in San Francisco. Probably around 1950.

(*Computer file: Helen Kleinert-001*)

Artifacts (*see page 45*)

This is an example of how I photograph and caption family artifacts.
I usually put this record in the appendix section of the book.

John Henry Moore's childhood chair. John was born December 3, 1859, in Fayette, Texas, and died December 17, 1935, in Temple, Texas. He is buried at the family gravesite at Bartlett Cemetery, Bartlett, Texas. This chair is now with Kristin Delaplane, his great-granddaughter, and is to be donated to The Republic of Texas Museum, 510 East Anderson Lane, Austin, Texas. The chair is made of wood and the seat is some type of animal hide. There is some wood damage from a California beetle. The chair has been treated and is now beetle free. It measures 13½" wide by 20" high.

Appendix D

Refer to Chapter Seven

Your Genealogy Record (*see page 49 et seq.*)

This is one of several free family tree charts you can obtain online at http://misbach.org/free-pdf-charts.html

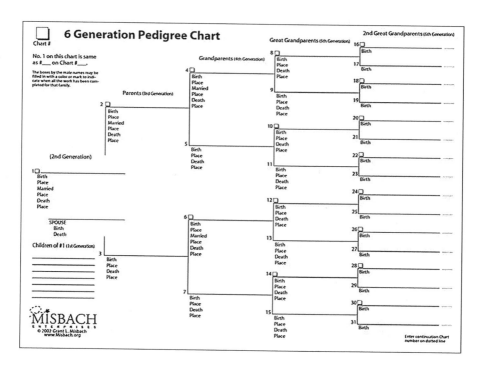

Captioning Your Source Documents (*see page 54*)

The following are examples of captioning primary sources.

1917–Death–John Caldwell Calhoun Moore–Santa Anna, Texas

Place of death Santa Anna, Coleman, Texas. White male, married. Date of death October 4, 1917, when he was 84 years old. Last seen by doctor on October 3. Cause of death cardiac degeneracy, senility, and acute coryza. He was a carpenter. Born in North Carolina. His father's name was Edwin Lewis Moore, also born in North Carolina. His mother's name was Elizabeth Lawson Hart, born in North Carolina. The person who gave the family information was R. D. Moore (John's son, Robert Diggs Moore) who lived in Fort Worth at 1952 Austin Avenue. John was buried in the Santa Anna Cemetery (Plot: Plat 1, Block 14).

1860 US Census—Jew Delaplane—Oronoko, Berrien, Michigan

Lines 6 thru 15: Household, Parents Benjamin F Delaplane age 44 born in Maryland was a physician and Harriet Delaplane age 42 born in Ohio. Children born in Indiana: Catherine J., 19; William H., 16; Harriet S., 14. Children born in Michigan: Sophia, 11; William F., 10; Jew, 8; Mary E., 2; Edwina, 5. William was the only one attending school. Benjamin had real estate valued at $1,200 and assets valued at $500. —Courtesy of Ancestry.com

How to Write Your Genealogy (*see page 56*)

> **The Hills**
>
> **Benjamin Hill** was born in 1699 in the state of Virginia. He died in 1799. Place of death unknown, but may have been in Pennsylvania. He was 100 years of age when he died. (*See stories of him on pp. 55–56.*)
>
> **Hardy Hill**, son of Benjamin, was born in 1754 in Virginia. In 1783, at age 29, he married Margaret Wallace, who was 23, in Derry, Westmoreland, Pennsylvania. Margaret was born in 1760 in Antrim Township, Franklin, Pennsylvania. Hardy and Margaret had eight children. Hardy died on December 17, 1798, in Salt River, Spencer, Kentucky. He was 44 years old. Margaret died in 1854 in Taylorsville, Shelby, Kentucky, at age 94. (See Hardy's story on page x.)
>
> **Isaac Hill**, first child for Hardy and Margaret, was born on December 22, 1784, in Kentucky. On April 16, 1807, at age 22, he married 19-year-old Margaret Cunningham in Shelby, Kentucky. Margaret was born on October 9, 1787, in Washington County, Pennsylvania. She is said to have been kin to author Lew Wallace, who wrote *Ben-Hur*. Isaac served in the military and was in the Battle of New Orleans, January 1815. Isaac and Margaret had 13 children. Isaac died at age 68 on February 11, 1853, in Clark County, Illinois. Margaret died a year later at age 67 on November 23, 1854. Place of death unknown.
>
> **John Berry Hill**, son of Isaac and Margaret, was their eleventh child. He was born on October 23, 1827, in Shelburn, Indiana. He married Mary Ann Wright, said to be a descendant of John Alden and Priscilla Mullins, passengers on the Mayflower. John and Mary married on May 23, 1853, in Prairietown, Indiana. John was 25 and Mary, who was born on May 23, 1853, in Prairietown, was 21. John and Mary had 11 children. John died at age 88 on February 7, 1916, in Charleston, Coles, Illinois. Mary died five years later at age 89 on March 18, 1921, also in Charleston. (See John's story on page xx.) (See Mary Ann Wright's branch of the family tree on page xxx.)

As with Mary Ann Wright, ancestral lines branch out with marriages. In this case, I steered the reader to a page where I have presented her ancestral line.

An Example of a Family History Narrative.

The Moores of Virginia and North Carolina

JAMES MOORE WAS THIRTY-SIX when the Revolutionary War broke out in 1776. He was said to be fervent in the cause; however, there is no record of how he may have participated in the action. He died in the midst of that war in 1778 at age thirty-eight. His son James was eleven years old at the out-break of the war. As soon as he reached the age of sixteen in 1781, he entered the war by going aboard a privateer schooner.

James Moore, the father, was born in 1740 in Southampton, Virginia. It has been passed down that the Moores had been set-tled in Virginia for some time before his birth. He was still living in Southampton when at age twenty he married seventeen-year-old Selah Williams, who was of Welsh origin.

The couple moved to Halifax, North Carolina, on land that today is in the hands of their descendants. The couple had three boys, John, James, and Jesse. Selah died in 1766 at age twenty-three, giving birth to Jesse. This was just six years after her wed-ding day and ten years before the start of the Revolutionary War. James remarried a year later to Elizabeth Pound. She and James had three daughters and one son.

When the son James entered the war, he shipped out on the *Hannah* for eight weeks. They sailed out of Edenton, North Car-olina, then put up in Beaufort, North Carolina, for repairs and after which they sailed to Charleston, South Carolina, where they took four ships as prizes. After his time at sea, James joined the army and was at Little York to see the surrender of Cornwallis. (see James's Revolutionary War recollections page xxx)

This James, who had served in the Revolutionary War, had three marriages. He married Martha Williams when he was twenty-two and she was seventeen. They had two children, a girl and a boy. Martha died at age twenty-three, just five months after giving birth to their son, Alfred. A year later, in 1794, James, who was then twenty-nine, married Sallie Ann Figures Lewis, twenty-five, a widow with four children. James and Sallie then had ten children, so it was a house-hold with fourteen children. Sallie died at age sixty-one. Five years after her death in 1835, James, then seventy, married sixty-five-year-old Mary Council. She died in 1849 and James died two years later, in 1851 at age eighty-six. He was buried along with his wives at the family farm cemetery in North Carolina, where many of those gravestones can be seen today.

Appendix E

Refer to Chapter Eight

Family Trees (*see page 59*)

Example of a pedigree chart

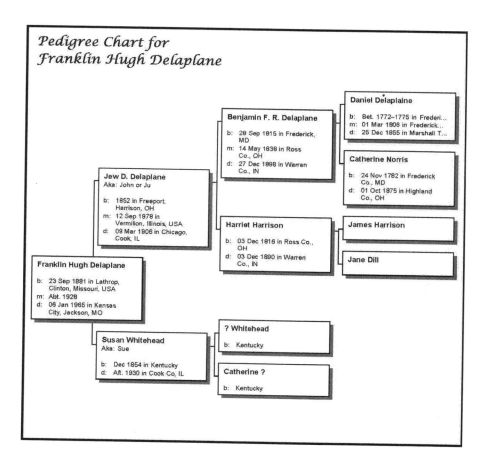

Pedigree Chart for
Franklin Hugh Delaplane

Daniel Delaplaine
b: Bet. 1772–1775 in Frederi...
m: 01 Mar 1806 in Frederick...
d: 25 Dec 1855 in Marshall T...

Benjamin F. R. Delaplane
b: 28 Sep 1815 in Frederick, MD
m: 14 May 1838 in Ross Co., OH
d: 27 Dec 1898 in Warren Co., IN

Catherine Norris
b: 24 Nov 1782 in Frederick Co., MD
d: 01 Oct 1875 in Highland Co., OH

Jew D. Delaplane
Aka: John or Ju
b: 1852 in Freeport, Harrison, OH
m: 12 Sep 1878 in Vermilion, Illinois, USA
d: 09 Mar 1906 in Chicago, Cook, IL

Harriet Harrison
b: 03 Dec 1816 in Ross Co., OH
d: 03 Dec 1890 in Warren Co., IN

James Harrison

Jane Dill

Franklin Hugh Delaplane
b: 23 Sep 1881 in Lathrop, Clinton, Missouri, USA
m: Abt. 1928
d: 06 Jan 1965 in Kansas City, Jackson, MO

? Whitehead
b: Kentucky

Susan Whitehead
Aka: Sue
b: Dec 1854 in Kentucky
d: Aft. 1930 in Cook Co, IL

Catherine ?
b: Kentucky

Example of a relationship chart

Relationship: Jew D. Delaplane to James Delaplaine

James Delaplaine is the 3rd great grandfather of Jew D. Delaplane

3rd great grandfather

James Delaplaine	Hannah Cock
b: 1660	b: 05 Aug 1669
New York, NY	Matinecock, Long Island, NY
d: 12 Apr 1750	d: 20 Jun 1755
Germantown, PA	Germantown, PA

2nd great grandfather

Joshua Delaplaine
b: 1706
Germantown, PA
d: 15 Feb 1788
Philadelphia, PA

Great grandfather

John Delaplaine
b: 1741
Berks Co., PA
d: 04 Jan 1804
Frederick Co., MD

Paternal grandfather

Daniel Delaplaine
b: Bet. 1772–1775
Frederick Co., MD
d: 25 Dec 1855
Marshall Twp., Highland, OH

Father

Benjamin F. R. Delaplane
b: 28 Sep 1815
Frederick, MD
d: 27 Dec 1898
Warren Co., IN

Self

Jew D. Delaplane
b: 1852
Freeport, Harrison, OH
d: 09 Mar 1906
Chicago, Cook, IL

Historical Backgrounds

This is an example of history background as a graphic element (*see page 60*).

A Brief History of Syracuse

The Erie Canal, which links the waters of Lake Erie in the west to the Hudson River in the east, opened in 1825, and, at that time, the canal ran through the center of Syracuse. The canal, and later the railroads, established Syracuse as an important transportation hub, and this, in turn, attracted a diverse number of manufacturing and commercial concerns. Salt manufacturing, which had been the main industry, declined, but Syracuse's many established businesses and diversified industries assured the city's continued economic prosperity. Candle makers, beer brewers, steel producers, and manufacturers of furniture, caskets, bicycles, and cars helped the city to flourish. All sorts of goods—gears, typewriters, electrical devices, shoes, glass, and china, to name just a few—were made in Syracuse by companies that took advantage of its good transportation system, its central location, and its ready, skilled labor force.

Examples of Timelines (*see page 61*)

Albert T. Henley Timeline		
Year	**Age**	**Event**
February 14, 1916		Birth: Grand Rapids, MI.
1922–25	6–9	Residence: Long Island, NY.
1925	9	Residence: Coronado, CA.
1926	10	Residence: Construction begins on house at Point Loma, CA.
1926–1934	9–17	School: Attends San Diego Army and Navy Military Academy as a boarder.
1933–1934	17–18	Travel: Europe
1934–1940	18–24	School: Stanford University and Stanford Law School.
1940–1945	24–29	Military: Counter Intelligence Core.
1947	31–	Occupation: Lawyer for the Santa Clara Water District, CA.
December 16, 1947	31	Marriage: Jesse Jean Host, CA
1948	32	Residence: Purchased house in Los Altos Hills, CA.

Delaplaine Family Timeline		
Year	**Age**	**Event**
1560		Birth: Jacques Delaplaine, Bressuire, Poitou,France.
1592		Birth: Nicholas Delaplaine, Bressuire, Poitou,France.
Jul 1, 1634		Birth: Nicholas Delaplaine, Bressuire, Poitou,France. (The Immigrant)
Sep 1, 1658	24	Marriage: Nicholas Delaplaine & Susanna Cresson (age 21), New Amsterdam (New York), NY.
1660		Birth: James Delaplaine, New York City, NY.
Aug 28, 1692	32	Marriage: James Delaplaine & Hannah Cock (age 23), Matinecock, Long Island, NY.
1697	104	Death: Nicholas Delaplaine, Bressuire, Poitou,France.
1706		Birth: Joshua Delaplaine, Germantown, PA.
1711	76	Death: Nicholas Delaplaine (The Immigrant), New York City, NY.
1739	33	Marriage: Joshua Delaplaine & Maria A. Shela(r) (age 21).
1741		Birth: John Delaplaine, Berks Co., PA.
Apr 12, 1750	90	Death: James Delaplaine, Germantown, PA.
1766	25	Marriage: John Delaplaine & Sophia Shelor (age 25), Berks Co., PA.
1775		Birth: Daniel Delaplaine, Frederick Co., MD.
Feb 15, 1788	82	Death: Joshua Delaplaine, Philadelphia, PA.
Jan 4, 1804	63	Death: John Delaplaine, Frederick Co., MD.
Mar 1, 1806	31	Marriage: Daniel Delaplaine & Catherine Norris (age 23), Frederick Co., MD

Conti—Gentiluomo Immigration Timeline		
Date	Age	Event
1904	44	Domenico Rositano of Sant'Eufemia d'Aspromonte, Reggio Calabria, Italy, immigrated to Lorain, OH.
About 1904	21	Carmello M. Conti immigrated to Bizerte, Tunisia.
1909	41	Angela Surace, wife of Domenico Rositano, and three children emigrated from Sant'Eufemia d'Aspromonte, Reggio Calabria, Italy.
1910	23	Vincenzo Gentiluomo emigrated from Sant'Eufemia d'Aspromonte, Reggio Calabria, Italy, to Cleveland, OH.
1917	44	Carmello M. Conti immigrated to Jamestown, NY from Bordeaux, France.
Before 1947	20	Lucien Conti, son of Joseph Conti, emigrated from Toulon, Allier, Auvergne, France, to Jamestown, NY.
1947	47	Joseph Conti, son of Carmello, emigrated from Toulon, Allier, Auvergne, France, to Jamestown, NY.

Appendix F

Self-Marketing

BEFORE THE INTERNET and the advent of eBooks, traditional publishers sold books by spending thousands of dollars on ad space in print media, such as the daily and Sunday *New York Times*; sending authors on expensive first-class tours to key cities for bookstore readings; and trying to place authors on evening talk shows like The *Tonight Show* with Jack Paar or Johnny Carson, or morning shows like the *Today Show*.

Today, book marketing is very different. Traditional publishers can't afford the old-fashioned publicity, and in any case, it doesn't work in today's market because readers find out about books through online media, social networking, and some reviews on television or in print journalism.

Consequently, whether you're published by Simon and Schuster or self-published, it's the author who is expected to and must, in fact, do all the heavy lifting.

That's why, in order to sell your memoir, whether it's about some other family member or yourself, you have to plan your own campaign. A book-marketing campaign needs to include:

Building a website. WordPress and other website-hosting companies provide excellent templates so you can do it yourself, or you can hire professionals who can help you do something a bit more attractive and original. This website should focus on the memoir itself, and can be launched long before the book is completed. You can use it to attract family members or perfect strangers to send in ideas and materials related to the content focus, period, and context of the subject. As you begin to assemble interviews, historical research, photographs, and other memorabilia, you can post some of it on this website and invite comment, or inspire additional ideas and donations. As you get further along, you can post sample scenes and chapters, and a clear link to the next crucial thing you should do. . . .

Starting a blog. You don't have to post something every day, but get one going and don't leave it for too long. This blog can be started, as with the website, long before the memoir is completed and be a kind of running journal or diary of your activities in writing the book. Eventually, you can tell your readers how to order the book.

Self-marketing has become a major field with several excellent websites and books you can consult for techniques, guidelines, and resources. Here are some I recommend.

- *APE: Author, Publisher, Entrepreneur* — How to Publish a Book by Guy Kawasaki and Shawn Welch. Nononina Press, 2012.

- *Dan Poynter's Self-Publishing Manual* and *Dan Poynter's Self-Publishing Manual, Volume 2*, by Dan Poynter Para Publishing, 1979–2003.

- *Dan Poynter's Writing Nonfiction*, by Dan Poynter, Para Publishing, 2000–2010.

- *The Self-Publisher's Ultimate Resource Guide* by Joel Friedlander and Betty Kelly Sargent. Marin Bookworks, 2014.

The field is changing rapidly, so new ideas and resources appear all the time. Stay current by reading about self-publishing and self-marketing online.

Appendix G

Further Reading

Carmack, Sharon DeBartolo. *Organizing Your Family History Search: Efficient and Effective Ways to Gather and Protect Your Genealogical Research*. Betterway Books, 1999.

Carmack, Sharon DeBartolo. *You Can Write Your Family History*. Genealogical Publishing Company, 2008.

Frazee, Hank. *Before We Say "Goodnight": How to Tell Bedtime Stories About Your Life and Family*. Morgan James Publishing, 2014.

Gouldrup, Lawrence P. *Writing the Family Narrative*. Ancestry, Inc., 1987.

Kanin, Ruth. *Write the Story of Your Life*. Clearfield Co., 1981.

Kempthorne, Charley. *For All Time: A Complete Guide to Writing Your Family History*. Heinemann, 1996.

Leclerc, Michael J. and Hoff, Henry B. (eds.). *Genealogical Writing in the 21st Century: A Guide to Register Style and More*. New England Historic Genealogical Society, 2006.

Levenick, Denise May. *How to Archive Family Keepsakes: Learn How to Preserve Family Photos, Memorabilia, and Genealogy Records*. Family Tree Books, 2012.

Stahel, Paula. *Listen Up: The Art of Interviewing for Personal History*. Breath and Shadows, 2013.

Sturdevant, Kathleen Scott. *Organizing and Preserving Your Heirloom Documents*. Betterway Books, 2002.

Williams, Don & Jaggar, Louisa. *Saving Stuff: How to Care for and Preserve Your Collectibles, Heirlooms, and Other Prized Possessions*. Touchstone, 2005.

About the Author

Biographer and personal historian Kristin Delaplane helps people capture their family or company stories through oral history interviews and historical and genealogy research. For many clients, the end result is carefully crafted as a narrative for an heirloom book. From the great American landscape, her clients have included notable families and celebrities, including Best Actor Oscar winners and a Kennedy Center Honoree. A number of these histories are now deposited in public archives.

Kristin's workshop on oral history methods has been featured with colleges and universities, high schools, museums, historical societies, and private organizations. An online course was featured with the University of California Extension at Davis for over eight years. Her project management and consultancy services have been employed by businesses such as San Francisco's famed Buena Vista Café and Genentech Corporation.

Named oral historian for the highly acclaimed Vacaville Museum in Solano County, California, Kristin initiated and oversaw a project involving over sixty oral histories that resulted in a museum exhibit and the publication of *Solano's Gold: The People and Their Orchards*, published in 1999.

Her newspaper feature on California history, "Echoes of Solano's Past," appeared in the award-winning *Vacaville Reporter* from 1995 through 1999. In 1998, a television documentary, co-produced, written, and narrated by Kristin won a Cablevision Award.

In 1998, Kristin published *A Gold Hunter: Memoirs of John Berry Hill*, based on her ancestor's California gold rush journal. The book was named an official California Sesquicentennial Resource.

From 1972 to 1993, Kristin was the inquiring photographer columnist for the *San Francisco Chronicle*. This column, "Question Man by Conti," garnered notable recognition including a day in San Francisco named for Kristin.

An interest in family history was sparked early on with fireside stories about her family heritage. She traces her American family back to 1609 at the Jamestown Colony, the Mayflower pilgrims John Alden and Priscilla Mullins (family lore that can't be proven, but seems probable), an ancestor who was captured and raised by Indians, and a grandmother, great-grandmother, and great-great-grandmother, all of whom survived the 1906 San Francisco earthquake.

Please visit our website at

www.ouramericanstories.com

We want to help you with your project.
See about our DIY sessions.

We are gathering readers' input for future editions.
We invite you to submit your success stories.
Tell us about any challenges you ran across and how you resolved them.

Our American Stories ® LLC

9363 N. Sunflower Blossom Place

Tucson, Arizona 85743-5196

Phone: (415) 515-9800

Email: kdelaplane@ouramericanstories.com

31920639R00061

Made in the USA
San Bernardino, CA
23 March 2016